UNDERSTANDING ARTIFICIAL INTELLIGENCE

James Lacroix
Understanding Artificial Intelligence: Past, Present, and Future

—

Published by - Spines
ISBN: 979-8-89691-287-3

Understanding Artificial Intelligence

Past, Present, and Future

James Lacroix

Contents

Introduction

In this 21st century, Artificial intelligence (AI) has become one of the most transformative technologies, which has been of great help in a whole lot of day to day aspect, in the reshaping industries, altering personal lifestyles, and challenging our understanding of intelligence itself.

Starting up from the smartphones we carry around, to the algorithms that power online recommendations.

It'll interest you to know that AI is all around us, and it even influences aspects of our daily lives.

Yet, despite its widespread presence, AI remains a mystery to many, wrapped in complex terminology and high-level concepts that can feel distant from everyday experiences. This book aims to bridge that gap, demystifying AI by explaining what it is, where it came from, and how it affects us today.

In order to understand AI, you need to know that AI isn't one single technology, but rather it's an umbrella term for a collection of tools and methods designed to mimic human cognitive abilities, such as learning, reasoning, and problem-solving. These capabilities allow AI to perform tasks that traditionally required human intelligence, from recognizing images and understanding spoken language to making complex predictions based on data. The development of AI has introduced tools like machine learning, neural networks, and deep learning, each adding new layers of capability to machines and pushing the boundaries of what's possible.

The origin of AI dates back to the mid-20th century, where it was rooted in early philosophical and scientific attempts to define intelligence. With key breakthroughs, such as the invention of the Turing Test and the creation of early expert systems, researchers laid the foundation for AI as we know it. Over the years, AI has faced periods of great progress and equally notable setbacks, often referred to as "AI winters" when funding and interest waned. However, recent advancements in computing power, data availability, and algorithmic techniques have led to a renaissance, bringing AI closer to realizing some of its long-held promises.

Today, AI technology permeates nearly every sector, from healthcare and education to finance and entertainment. It powers personal assistants like Siri and Alexa, enhances medical diagnoses, automates repetitive business processes, and even drives autonomous vehicles. With such varied applications, the influence of AI extends across individual, educational, and corporate domains, transforming how we interact, learn, and work. However, alongside its benefits, AI also presents ethical questions about privacy, security, and the future of employment, making it essential for everyone to understand its impacts.

Looking to the future, AI holds the potential to unlock solutions to some of humanity's greatest challenges, from climate change to global health. At the same time, concerns about AI's potential misuse or unregulated development are prompting global discussions on responsible AI governance. This book will explore not only the potential and current uses of AI but also the considerations and responsibilities that come with it.

Whether you're curious about how AI affects your personal life, interested in how it's transforming education, or looking to understand its role in modern business, this book will provide a comprehensive guide. By the end, you'll have a foundational understanding of AI's core concepts, its history, and its possibilities—both for now and in the years to come. With this knowledge, you'll be better equipped to navigate an AI-driven world, making informed decisions about how to engage with and benefit from this powerful technology.

CHAPTER 1

WHAT IS ARTIFICIAL INTELLIGENCE?

In recent years, Artificial Intelligence (AI) has become a buzzword, but in order to understand its true meaning, it requires delving deeper into its definitions, its types, and foundational concepts.

Despite its growing ubiquity, AI remains a complex and often misunderstood field. This chapter will clarify what AI is, its different types, and the key concepts underpinning its development, including machine learning, deep learning, and neural networks. Additionally, we will explore the distinctions between AI, machine learning, and data science to offer a comprehensive understanding.

DEFINITIONS AND TYPES OF AI

Artificial intelligence at its core, refers to the machine capability to perform tasks that typically require human intelligence. These tasks include learning from experience, understanding language, recognizing patterns, solving problems, and making decisions. AI systems are designed to mimic cognitive functions that we associate with the human mind, such as reasoning, learning, problem-solving, perception, and language understanding.

Artificial intelligence is quite broad, but it can be categorized into three main types, based on its capabilities. Narrow AI, general AI and superintelligent AI.

1. Narrow AI (Weak AI): The most common form of AI in our today world. Narrow AI is designed to perform specific tasks within a limited scope. These systems are highly specialized and excel in their designated functions, such as facial recognition, language translation, or playing chess. However, they lack generalization abilities beyond their trained tasks. For example, while an AI-powered chatbot might be able to converse with you about travel plans, it cannot suddenly start diagnosing medical conditions or autonomously drive a car without specific programming for those tasks.

2. General AI (Strong AI): General AI refers to a hypothetical form of AI that possesses the ability to understand, learn, and apply knowledge across a wide range of tasks, much like a human being. It would be capable of independent problem-solving and could transfer knowledge from one domain to another. While current AI technologies have made impressive strides, we have yet to develop systems that exhibit true general AI capabilities. Achieving

this would require machines to exhibit human-like understanding, consciousness, and reasoning, which remain theoretical concepts as of now.

3. Superintelligent AI: This represents a level of intelligence that surpasses human cognitive abilities. Superintelligent AI would not only perform tasks with superhuman efficiency but also potentially understand concepts and solve problems that are currently beyond human comprehension. The idea of superintelligent AI raises significant ethical and existential questions, as it could lead to scenarios where AI systems surpass human control. However, this level of AI remains speculative and is the subject of ongoing debates among researchers and ethicists.

Key Concepts in AI: Machine Learning, Deep Learning, and Neural Networks

To understand the mechanics behind AI, it involves exploring key concepts, such as machine learning, deep learning and neutral networks. These are the building blocks that has driven the recent surge in AI capabilities and applications.

1. Machine Learning: Machine learning (ML) is a subset of AI that enables systems to learn from data and improve over time without being explicitly programmed. Traditional programming involves writing explicit instructions for a computer to follow, but machine learning allows

systems to identify patterns in large datasets and make predictions or decisions based on those patterns. The core idea behind ML is that a model can be trained on a dataset to recognize patterns and make accurate predictions on new, unseen data.

Machine learning can be categorized into three main types:

- Supervised Learning: In supervised learning, the model is trained on a labeled dataset, where each input has a corresponding correct output. The algorithm learns by comparing its predictions with the actual labels and adjusting its parameters to minimize errors. Common applications include spam detection, image classification, and predictive analytics.
- Unsupervised Learning: Unsupervised learning involves training a model on data without explicit labels. The algorithm tries to identify hidden patterns or groupings within the data. Clustering (e.g., customer segmentation) and dimensionality reduction (e.g., data visualization) are common examples of unsupervised learning techniques.
- Reinforcement Learning: In reinforcement learning, an agent learns by interacting with its environment and receiving feedback in the form of rewards or penalties. The goal is to learn a policy that maximizes cumulative rewards over time. Reinforcement learning is widely used in robotics, gaming, and autonomous vehicles.

1. Deep Learning: Deep learning is a specialized subset of machine learning that uses neural networks with multiple layers (hence the term "deep") to process and analyze data. Deep learning has gained prominence due to its success in handling complex tasks like image and speech recognition, natural language processing, and even beating human champions in games like Go.

The structure of deep learning models allows them to automatically extract features from raw data, eliminating the need for manual feature engineering. For example, in image recognition, a deep learning model can learn to identify edges, shapes, and objects in images without human intervention. The depth of the network, or the number of layers, is a key factor in its ability to capture intricate patterns in data.

1. Neural Networks: Neural networks are the fundamental building blocks of deep learning models. Inspired by the structure of the human brain, neural networks consist of interconnected nodes (neurons) organized into layers. Each neuron receives input, processes it using a mathematical function, and passes the output to the next layer. The network adjusts its parameters (weights and biases) during training to minimize the difference between predicted and actual outputs.

There are various types of neural networks, each suited for different tasks:

- Convolutional Neural Networks (CNNs): CNNs are primarily used for image and video processing. They can automatically detect patterns such as edges, textures, and shapes in visual data.
- Recurrent Neural Networks (RNNs): RNNs are designed for sequential data, such as time series or natural language text. They have memory mechanisms that allow them to retain information from previous inputs, making them effective for tasks like language translation and speech recognition.
- Generative Adversarial Networks (GANs): GANs consist of two neural networks—a generator and a discriminator—that compete against each other. GANs are used to generate realistic images, videos, and even deepfake content.

THE DIFFERENCE BETWEEN AI, MACHINE LEARNING, AND DATA SCIENCE

As much as AI, machine learning and data science, are often used interchangeably, they also are distinct fields with different focuses;

1. Artificial Intelligence (AI): AI is the overarching field concerned with creating machines that can mimic human intelligence. It encompasses a wide range of techniques and applications, including machine learning, expert systems, robotics, and natural language processing.

2. Machine Learning (ML): ML is a subset of AI that focuses specifically on developing algorithms that allow machines to learn from and make predictions based on data. It is one of the primary methods used to achieve AI capabilities, enabling systems to improve automatically through experience.

3. Data Science: Data science is a broader discipline that involves extracting insights and knowledge from data using a combination of statistical analysis, machine learning, and data visualization. While AI and ML are often part of data science projects, the field also includes other techniques for analyzing and interpreting data, such as traditional statistical methods. Data scientists typically use machine learning as one of many tools to solve specific problems, while their focus is on understanding data patterns and trends.

In summary, AI is the broader concept of machines simulating human intelligence, machine learning is a method to achieve AI through data-driven learning, and data science is the interdisciplinary field that encompasses methods (including machine learning) to analyze data and extract insights.

Artificial intelligence is a rapidly evolving field with broad applications across various sectors. Understanding the distinctions between AI, machine learning, and data science, as well as key concepts like deep learning and neural networks, provides a foundation for exploring how these technologies shape our world. As we continue to develop AI systems with increasing capabilities, the line between human and machine intelligence becomes ever more blurred, offering exciting opportunities and presenting new challenges. The next chapter will delve into the history of AI, tracing its roots and the key developments that have led to the present state of this transformative technology.

CHAPTER 2

———————————

THE HISTORY OF AI

In this chapter, we will explore the early beginnings of AI, the major milestones, the infamous "AI winters," and the significant advancements that have shaped modern AI as we know it today.

The artificial intelligence story, is one which quips the human curiosity and ambition, also fueled by a desire to create machines that learn, think and reason like humans.

From its early inspirations in ancient myths to the rapid technological advancements of the 21st century, the history of AI is filled with breakthroughs, setbacks, and periods of intense exploration. This chapter explores the early beginnings of AI, major milestones, the infamous "AI winters," and the significant advancements that have shaped modern AI as we know it today.

Early Beginnings and Inspirations for AI

The idea of creating intelligent machines is not new; it has deep roots in ancient mythology, literature, and early mechanical inventions. Greek mythology features tales of automatons like Talos, a giant bronze warrior who protected Crete, and the legend of the Golem in Jewish folklore, a humanoid creature made from clay brought to life by mystical means. These stories reflect humanity's long-standing fascination with the concept of artificial life and intelligence.

In the 17th and 18th centuries, mechanical devices like the "Automaton" by Wolfgang von Kempelen—a chess-playing machine that was eventually revealed to be a hoax—captured the public's imagination. More scientifically grounded, mathematician and philosopher Blaise Pascal developed the Pascaline, an early mechanical calculator capable of performing basic arithmetic. These early mechanical devices laid the groundwork for thinking about machines that could mimic human cognitive functions.

The 20th century marked the formalization of many foundational ideas in AI. In 1950, British mathematician Alan Turing published his landmark paper, "Computing Machinery and Intelligence," introducing the concept of a machine that could simulate any human cognitive process. Turing proposed the famous "Turing Test," a method for determining whether a machine could exhibit behavior indistinguishable from that of a human. The Turing Test remains a fundamental concept in AI research, even as modern AI systems continue to challenge its premises.

Major Milestones in AI Development

The formal birth of AI as a field of study is often traced to the 1956 Dartmouth Conference, organized by computer scientists John McCarthy, Marvin Minsky, Nathaniel Rochester, and Claude Shannon. During this conference, McCarthy coined the term "artificial intelligence," proposing that "every aspect of learning or any other feature of intelligence can, in principle, be so precisely described that a machine can be made to simulate it." This ambitious vision set the stage for decades of research and development in AI.

In the 1960s and 1970s, early AI research focused on developing symbolic AI or "good old-fashioned AI" (GOFAI). Researchers believed that by encoding knowledge and rules explicitly, machines could mimic human reasoning. One of the first successful AI programs was the Logic Theorist, developed by Allen Newell and Herbert A. Simon in 1955. The program was designed to prove mathematical theorems, and it successfully proved 38 of the first 52 theorems in Whitehead and Russell's Principia Mathematica. This was a significant milestone, demonstrating the potential of AI to tackle complex logical problems.

Another early AI system, ELIZA, was developed in the mid-1960s by Joseph Weizenbaum. ELIZA was an early natural language processing program that simulated a conversation with a psychotherapist by responding to user inputs with pre-defined scripts. Although ELIZA was relatively simple, its ability to mimic human conversation sparked widespread interest in AI's potential for language understanding.

In the 1980s, expert systems became a popular area of AI research. These systems used rule-based logic to simulate the decision-making processes of human experts in specific domains, such as medical diagnosis or financial analysis. One of the most notable expert systems was MYCIN, an AI program developed at Stanford University for diagnosing bacterial infections and recommending antibiotics. MYCIN's success demonstrated the practical utility of AI in solving specialized, knowledge-intensive tasks.

AI Winters and Revivals

Despite early successes, AI research faced significant challenges, leading to periods known as "AI winters." An AI winter refers to a period when enthusiasm, funding, and research in AI significantly decline due to unmet expectations and technical limitations.

The first AI winter occurred in the 1970s and early 1980s. Researchers had overestimated the capabilities of symbolic AI systems, believing that encoding human knowledge explicitly would lead to rapid advancements. However, these systems struggled with tasks that required understanding the nuances of language, perception, and real-world reasoning. The limitations of early AI, combined with economic factors, led to reduced funding and interest.

The revival of AI began in the mid-1980s with the development of new approaches, including neural networks and machine learning. Researchers realized that rather than explicitly programming rules, it was more effective to enable machines to learn from data. The emergence of backpropagation, a method for training neural networks, was a crucial breakthrough that reignited interest in AI.

A second AI winter occurred in the late 1980s and early 1990s. The hype surrounding expert systems had subsided as they failed to scale beyond narrow, specialized applications. Funding once again declined, and AI research faced skepticism from the broader scientific community.

However, the late 1990s marked another turning point as computing power increased and large datasets became more accessible. The development of support vector machines and advancements in probabilistic reasoning helped AI researchers tackle previously intractable problems. This period laid the groundwork for the AI renaissance of the 21st century.

Significant Breakthroughs in the 21st Century

The 21st century has seen an explosion of advancements in AI, driven by the convergence of big data, powerful computing, and innovative algorithms. One of the most significant breakthroughs came in 2012, when a deep learning model developed by Geoffrey Hinton and his team at the University of Toronto achieved a major victory in the ImageNet competition, a large-scale visual recognition challenge. Their model, based on a deep convolutional neural network (CNN), drastically reduced the error rate in image classification tasks and demonstrated the power of deep learning.

Another landmark achievement occurred in 2016 when Google DeepMind's AlphaGo defeated Lee Sedol, one of the world's top Go players. Go is an ancient board game with more possible moves than atoms in the observable universe, making it a complex challenge for AI. AlphaGo's victory was a testament to the advances in deep learning and reinforcement learning, showcasing AI's ability to handle strategic thinking and decision-making at an unprecedented level.

In natural language processing, OpenAI's GPT-3, released in 2020, represented a significant leap forward. GPT-3 is a transformer-based language model capable of understanding and generating human-like text based on prompts. It demonstrated a remarkable ability to perform tasks such as language translation, summarization, and even creative writing, showcasing the potential of AI to revolutionize how we interact with technology.

The rapid growth of AI in the 21st century has been accompanied by widespread adoption across industries. AI is now a critical tool in healthcare, where it aids in diagnosing diseases, predicting patient outcomes, and accelerating drug discovery. In finance, AI algorithms detect fraud, automate trading, and provide personalized financial advice. Autonomous vehicles, powered by AI, are beginning to revolutionize transportation, while AI-driven recommendation systems enhance user experiences on platforms like Netflix, Amazon, and Spotify.

The history of AI is a tale of human ingenuity, marked by moments of triumph, periods of disillusionment, and persistent innovation. From the early dreams of creating intelligent machines to the significant breakthroughs of the 21st century, AI has evolved into a transformative technology shaping the future of humanity. The field has moved beyond symbolic reasoning and expert systems to embrace machine learning, deep learning, and neural networks, unlocking new possibilities in perception, language understanding, and autonomous decision-making.

As we continue to advance in AI research, the potential applications seem limitless. However, the journey is far from over, and new challenges and ethical considerations lie ahead. The next chapter will explore the current state of AI, examining its capabilities, limitations, and the role it plays in shaping our modern world.

CHAPTER 3

THE CURRENT STATE OF AI

Artificial Intelligence (AI) has become one of the most transformative technologies of the 21st century, rapidly evolving from a speculative concept to a tool that permeates nearly every industry. From the rise of autonomous vehicles to chatbots that can hold conversations almost indistinguishable from human interactions, the current state of AI showcases its remarkable capabilities. This chapter provides an overview of contemporary AI technologies, the key players driving innovation, recent breakthroughs, and the ethical challenges that accompany this rapid advancement.

OVERVIEW OF CURRENT AI TECHNOLOGIES AND CAPABILITIES

AI technologies today span a vast array of applications, from voice assistants like Siri and Alexa to sophisticated algorithms that can detect diseases in medical images. The following are some key areas where AI is currently making significant impacts:

1. Natural Language Processing (NLP): NLP enables machines to understand, interpret, and respond to human language. Modern NLP systems can perform tasks such as text translation, sentiment analysis, and content generation. Large language models like OpenAI's GPT-4 and Google's BERT have set new standards in understanding and generating human language. These models can answer questions, generate essays, and even engage in complex conversations with humans, making NLP one of the most visible applications of AI in everyday life.

2. Computer Vision: This area of AI focuses on enabling machines to interpret and understand visual information from the world. Advances in deep learning, particularly convolutional neural networks (CNNs), have made computer vision a powerful tool for image and video recognition, facial recognition, and even object detection in real-time. Applications include autonomous driving, where AI systems identify road signs, pedestrians, and other vehicles, as well as healthcare, where AI can detect anomalies in medical scans.

3. Robotics and Automation: AI has played a pivotal role in advancing robotics, enabling machines to perform complex tasks that require dexterity, precision, and decision-making capabilities. Robots powered by AI are increasingly used in

manufacturing, logistics, and even healthcare, where they can perform surgeries with high precision. In autonomous vehicles, AI systems combine computer vision, sensor data, and machine learning to navigate safely and efficiently.

4. Recommendation Systems: These AI-driven systems analyze vast amounts of user data to make personalized suggestions. Companies like Netflix, Amazon, and YouTube use recommendation algorithms to enhance user experiences by suggesting relevant movies, products, or videos. These systems rely on machine learning techniques to predict what a user might be interested in based on their previous interactions and preferences.

5. Generative AI: Generative AI, exemplified by models like DALL-E and Midjourney, can create images, music, text, and even 3D models from user inputs. These models use deep learning architectures, such as Generative Adversarial Networks (GANs) and transformers, to produce realistic and creative outputs. Generative AI is being explored in various industries, from entertainment and marketing to design and product development.

KEY PLAYERS AND ORGANIZATIONS IN AI

Several companies and organizations are at the forefront of AI research and development, each contributing to the field's rapid growth. Here are some of the most influential entities:

1. Google DeepMind: DeepMind, a subsidiary of Alphabet Inc., is renowned for its groundbreaking work in AI. It gained global recognition in 2016 when its AlphaGo program defeated world champion Lee Sedol in the game of Go, a significant milestone in AI development. DeepMind continues to push the boundaries with research in reinforcement learning, healthcare, and AI ethics.

2. OpenAI: Founded with the mission to ensure that artificial general intelligence (AGI) benefits all of humanity, OpenAI has been a leader in developing cutting-edge language models like GPT-3 and GPT-4. These models have set new benchmarks in natural language understanding and generation, demonstrating capabilities that range from writing coherent essays to generating creative content.

3. Microsoft: Microsoft has made significant investments in AI, integrating it across its suite of products, such as Azure AI, and collaborating with OpenAI to bring advanced language models to its cloud services. Its AI research focuses on enhancing productivity, developing responsible AI, and advancing areas like machine learning and computer vision.

4. IBM Watson: IBM's Watson was one of the first AI systems to gain widespread attention for its victory on the game show Jeopardy! in 2011. Watson has since evolved into a versatile AI platform that offers solutions in healthcare, finance, and customer

service. IBM's focus on explainable AI and ethical AI development sets it apart in the industry.

5. NVIDIA: Known for its powerful graphics processing units (GPUs), NVIDIA plays a crucial role in AI research and deployment. Its hardware is essential for training deep learning models, and the company has expanded into software development with AI frameworks like CUDA and cuDNN. NVIDIA's GPUs have become the backbone of modern AI infrastructure.

6. Amazon and Meta (Facebook): Both Amazon and Meta have invested heavily in AI, focusing on enhancing user experiences, streamlining operations, and innovating in emerging fields like augmented reality (AR) and virtual reality (VR). Amazon's AI-driven recommendation engine and Meta's advancements in AI-powered content moderation and computer vision are just a few examples of their contributions.

RECENT BREAKTHROUGHS IN AI

The past few years have seen several remarkable advancements in AI across various domains:

1. Natural Language Processing (NLP): The development of transformer-based models like GPT-4 and BERT has revolutionized NLP. These models can perform tasks such as text completion, translation, and summarization with unprecedented accuracy. Their ability to generate

human-like responses has opened new possibilities in customer service, content creation, and education.

2. Image Recognition and Computer Vision: Advances in deep learning have significantly improved the accuracy of image recognition systems. Applications such as facial recognition, medical imaging, and autonomous vehicle navigation have benefited from these improvements. Google's DeepMind recently developed an AI model capable of diagnosing over 50 eye diseases from retinal scans, showcasing the potential of AI in healthcare.

3. Robotics: AI has enhanced robotics, making them more capable of complex tasks. Boston Dynamics, for instance, has developed robots like Spot and Atlas, which can navigate rough terrain, dance, and even perform parkour. These advancements demonstrate the potential of AI-powered robots in disaster response, logistics, and industrial applications.

4. AI in Drug Discovery: AI has made significant strides in healthcare, particularly in drug discovery. Companies like DeepMind and Insilico Medicine use AI to identify potential drug candidates and predict their efficacy. The rapid development of COVID-19 vaccines, supported by AI-driven research, highlighted the technology's potential to accelerate drug discovery processes.

Ethical Considerations, Bias in AI, and Responsible AI Development

As AI technologies advance, so do concerns about their ethical implications. Key issues include bias in AI algorithms, privacy concerns, and the potential for misuse.

1. Bias in AI: AI systems can perpetuate and even amplify biases present in their training data. For example, facial recognition algorithms have shown higher error rates for people of color, leading to concerns about racial bias and discrimination. Addressing bias in AI requires diverse datasets, careful model evaluation, and inclusive design practices.

2. Privacy Concerns: The ability of AI systems to collect, analyze, and infer information from large datasets raises significant privacy issues. Companies and governments using AI for surveillance or data analysis can inadvertently infringe on individual privacy rights. Ensuring data protection and developing transparent AI systems are crucial steps in mitigating these concerns.

3. Job Displacement: Automation powered by AI has the potential to replace certain jobs, particularly those involving repetitive tasks. While AI can create new opportunities, it also poses a challenge for workers in industries vulnerable to automation. Policymakers and companies must work together to retrain the workforce and prepare for the evolving job market.

4. Responsible AI Development: As AI becomes more powerful, there is a growing need for ethical guidelines to ensure its responsible development. Initiatives like the AI Ethics Guidelines by the European Union and research efforts from organizations like the Partnership on AI focus on promoting fairness, transparency, and accountability in AI systems.

The current state of AI is marked by rapid advancements and widespread adoption across various sectors. From natural language processing to robotics, AI's capabilities are expanding, driven by key players and groundbreaking innovations. However, the rise of AI also brings ethical challenges that must be addressed to ensure its responsible and fair use. As we move forward, understanding the balance between leveraging AI's potential and mitigating its risks will be crucial in shaping its impact on society. The next chapter will delve into AI's applications in everyday life, exploring how it is transforming personal, educational, and business experiences.

Chapter 4

Personal Use Cases of AI

Artificial Intelligence (AI) has become an integral part of our daily lives, often in ways we may not even realize. From personalized recommendations on streaming platforms to virtual assistants that help manage our schedules, AI is embedded in numerous applications, making our lives more convenient and efficient. This chapter explores how AI is used in everyday life, its role in health and wellness, and practical tips for leveraging AI tools to boost productivity and convenience.

AI in Everyday Life

AI has seamlessly integrated into our everyday activities, enhancing how we interact with technology and the world around us. Here are some of the most common ways AI impacts our daily routines:

1. Virtual Assistants:

Virtual assistants like Siri, Google Assistant, and Alexa are among the most visible examples of AI in personal use. These AI-powered tools use natural language processing (NLP) to understand voice commands, answer questions, play music, set reminders, and control smart home devices. By learning from user interactions, they become more adept at predicting needs and personalizing responses.

2. Recommendation Systems:

Recommendation systems are ubiquitous in the digital age. Platforms like Netflix, YouTube, Amazon, and Spotify utilize AI algorithms to analyze user behavior and preferences, providing personalized recommendations for movies, products, or music. These systems use machine learning to predict what content users will likely enjoy, increasing user engagement and satisfaction.

3. Smart Home Devices:

AI-powered smart home devices have transformed how we manage household tasks. Products like smart thermostats (e.g., Nest), smart lights (e.g., Philips Hue), and smart speakers (e.g., Amazon Echo) use AI to learn user preferences and automate home functions. For instance, a smart thermostat can learn your schedule and adjust the temperature accordingly, optimizing energy usage and increasing comfort.

4. Social Media:

Social media platforms such as Facebook, Instagram, and Twitter rely on AI to enhance user experiences. AI algorithms analyze user interactions, preferences, and engagement to curate personalized content feeds. Additionally, AI is used to filter out inappropriate content, detect fake news, and provide targeted advertising, tailoring the user experience to individual interests.

5. Navigation and Travel:

AI has significantly improved navigation tools like Google Maps and Waze. These apps use machine learning algorithms to analyze real-time traffic data, predict travel times, and suggest the fastest routes. AI also powers ride-hailing services like Uber and Lyft, matching passengers with drivers, estimating fares, and optimizing routes for efficiency.

HEALTH AND WELLNESS

The role of AI in health and wellness has expanded rapidly, offering innovative solutions that help individuals monitor their health, maintain fitness, and improve overall well-being. Here are some key areas where AI is making a significant impact:

1. Fitness Trackers and Wearable Devices:

AI-powered wearable devices like Fitbit, Apple Watch, and Garmin use sensors to collect data on physical activity, heart rate, sleep patterns, and more. These devices analyze the data using machine learning algorithms to provide insights into your health and fitness. For instance, they can track your daily steps, monitor your sleep quality, and even detect irregular heart rhythms. By offering personalized recommendations, they help users set goals and make informed decisions about their health.

2. Mental Health Apps:

AI-driven mental health apps like Woebot and Wysa use NLP and machine learning to provide mental health support. These chatbots engage users in conversations to help them manage stress, anxiety, and depression. By using AI to analyze user inputs, these apps can offer coping strategies, mindfulness exercises, and other therapeutic interventions. While not a replacement for professional therapy, these tools provide accessible and convenient support for individuals seeking to improve their mental well-being.

3. Nutrition and Diet Planning:

AI applications are increasingly used in diet and nutrition planning. Apps like MyFitnessPal and Lose It! leverage AI to track food intake, suggest healthy recipes, and provide insights into nutritional habits. By analyzing user data, these apps can offer personalized recommendations for achieving specific health goals, such as weight loss or muscle gain.

4. Telemedicine and Virtual Health Assistants:

The rise of telemedicine has been accelerated by AI technologies that enhance remote healthcare services. Virtual health assistants like Babylon Health and Ada Health use AI to assess symptoms, suggest possible conditions, and recommend next steps. By analyzing user-reported symptoms and medical history, these apps help individuals make informed decisions about seeking medical care.

Tips on Leveraging AI Tools for Productivity and Convenience

AI tools can significantly enhance productivity and make daily tasks more convenient. Here are some practical tips on how to leverage these technologies effectively:

1. Automate Routine Tasks with Virtual Assistants:

Virtual assistants like Siri, Alexa, and Google Assistant can help automate routine tasks, saving time and effort. You can set up reminders, schedule meetings, send texts, and even control smart home devices using voice commands. For example, you can ask your assistant to play music, turn off the lights, or remind you of an upcoming appointment, streamlining your daily activities.

2. Use AI-Powered Productivity Apps:

Several AI-powered apps can boost productivity by automating repetitive tasks and improving time management. Tools like Grammarly use AI to assist with writing, offering suggestions for grammar, clarity, and style, making your emails and documents more polished. Apps like Otter.ai provide automatic transcription services, converting speech into text, which is particularly useful for meeting notes or interviews.

Additionally, AI-driven project management tools like Trello and Asana can help you organize tasks, set deadlines, and collaborate with team members more effectively. By analyzing your work patterns, these apps can offer insights and suggest ways to optimize your workflow.

3. Enhance Your Learning with AI Educational Tools:

AI has revolutionized the way we learn and acquire new skills. Platforms like Duolingo and Khan Academy use machine learning algorithms to tailor lessons based on individual progress and learning speed. These adaptive learning systems adjust the difficulty of exercises based on your performance, providing a personalized learning experience.

For those looking to enhance their skills, AI-powered language models like ChatGPT can be valuable resources. You can use these models to ask questions, get explanations, or brainstorm ideas, making them useful study companions.

4. Optimize Your Finances with AI Financial Tools:

AI tools can help you manage your finances by offering personalized advice, tracking spending, and automating investments. Apps like Mint and PocketGuard analyze your financial data to provide insights into your spending habits, suggest budgeting strategies, and alert you to potential savings.

Robo-advisors like Betterment and Wealthfront use AI algorithms to create and manage investment portfolios based on your financial goals and risk tolerance. By automating the investment process, these tools make it easier for individuals to grow their wealth without extensive financial knowledge.

5. Stay Healthy with AI-Powered Wellness Apps:

Health and wellness apps powered by AI can help you maintain a healthy lifestyle. For example, fitness apps like Freeletics use AI to create customized workout plans based on your fitness level and goals. Meditation apps like Calm and Headspace leverage AI to offer personalized mindfulness exercises that cater to your stress levels and preferences.

By using these apps regularly, you can track your progress, set realistic goals, and receive personalized recommendations to enhance your well-being.

6. Improve Home Security with AI:

AI-driven home security systems provide enhanced protection for your home. Devices like Ring cameras and Nest security systems use AI to detect unusual activity, recognize faces, and send alerts to your smartphone. These systems can distinguish between different types of movements, such as a passing car or a person approaching your front door, reducing false alarms and increasing the accuracy of alerts.

AI's presence in our everyday lives is steadily growing, offering a wide range of tools and applications that enhance convenience, productivity, and well-being. Whether through virtual assistants that streamline our schedules, fitness trackers that monitor our health, or financial apps that help us manage our budgets, AI has become a valuable companion in managing daily tasks.

The integration of AI in personal use cases demonstrates its potential to make life easier and more efficient. As these technologies continue to evolve, we can expect even more innovative applications that cater to individual needs and preferences. By embracing AI tools and learning how to use them effectively, individuals can unlock new levels of productivity, enhance their well-being, and simplify their daily routines.

In the next chapter, we will explore the educational applications of AI, examining how this technology is transforming the way we learn, teach, and acquire new skills. From personalized learning platforms to intelligent tutoring systems, AI is shaping the future of education, making it more accessible, efficient, and tailored to individual needs.

CHAPTER 5

EDUCATIONAL APPLICATIONS OF AI

Artificial Intelligence (AI) is revolutionizing the education sector, offering new tools and methods to enhance teaching and learning experiences. From personalized online learning platforms to AI-driven research tools, this chapter explores the various educational applications of AI, its impact on skill development, and how educators can leverage these technologies to prepare students for the future job market.

AI in Classrooms and Online Learning Platforms

In traditional classrooms and online learning environments, AI is playing an increasingly significant role in transforming how education is delivered. The use of AI in education can be seen in various formats, from adaptive learning systems to intelligent tutoring.

1. Adaptive Learning Systems:

Adaptive learning systems use AI algorithms to tailor educational content to individual students' needs. These systems continuously analyze a student's performance, identify areas of weakness, and adjust the difficulty of exercises accordingly. For example, platforms like Khan Academy and Coursera use AI to recommend lessons or quizzes based on a learner's progress. This personalized approach helps students learn at their own pace, improving comprehension and retention.

2. Intelligent Tutoring Systems (ITS):

Intelligent tutoring systems are AI-powered programs that provide personalized guidance and feedback to students. These systems simulate one-on-one tutoring by understanding a student's responses and offering hints or explanations to help them grasp complex concepts. Examples include platforms like Carnegie Learning, which offers personalized math tutoring, and IBM's Watson Tutor, which provides assistance in various subjects. ITS helps bridge the gap between traditional classroom teaching and individualized instruction, making learning more interactive and effective.

3. Virtual Classrooms and AI-Enhanced Learning Tools:

The rise of virtual classrooms has accelerated the adoption of AI-powered tools that facilitate interactive learning. For instance, AI can be used to transcribe lectures in real-time, making it easier for students to follow along and review materials later. Additionally, AI can analyze student participation in online discussions, identifying patterns and providing insights to instructors about engagement levels.

Virtual teaching assistants, like Jill Watson from Georgia Tech, are AI-powered chatbots that help answer student questions, provide resources, and assist with administrative tasks. These tools not only enhance the learning experience but also free up time for educators to focus on more complex teaching activities.

AI in Research and Academic Support

AI is reshaping academic research by offering powerful tools that enhance data analysis, streamline literature reviews, and support experimental design. The following are key ways in which AI is assisting researchers and students:

1. Data Analysis and Visualization:

AI algorithms can analyze vast datasets quickly and accurately, making it easier for researchers to identify trends, correlations, and patterns. Tools like IBM's Watson and Google's AutoML allow researchers to use machine learning without needing extensive programming knowledge. These platforms enable researchers to build predictive models, conduct complex analyses, and visualize data in meaningful ways.

For example, in social sciences, AI can be used to analyze large volumes of survey data, identifying significant patterns and drawing insights that would be challenging to detect manually. In scientific research, AI-powered tools like Deep-Mind's AlphaFold have made significant contributions by predicting protein structures, accelerating discoveries in biochemistry and medicine.

2. Automated Literature Reviews:

Conducting a thorough literature review is a time-consuming process that requires sifting through hundreds of academic papers. AI tools like Semantic Scholar and Iris.ai use natural language processing (NLP) to scan vast databases of academic publications, identify relevant studies, and summarize key findings. These tools help researchers stay up-to-date with the latest developments in their fields, saving time and improving the quality of their reviews.

3. Academic Writing Assistance:

AI-powered writing tools like Grammarly and Turnitin provide valuable support for students and researchers by offering real-time feedback on grammar, style, and originality. Grammarly uses NLP algorithms to suggest improvements, making academic writing clearer and more professional. Turnitin's plagiarism detection software analyzes submissions against a vast database of academic content, ensuring the integrity of research work.

Additionally, AI-driven tools like QuillBot and ChatGPT assist in paraphrasing, summarizing, and generating ideas for academic papers, helping students overcome writer's block and enhance the quality of their writing.

The Role of AI in Developing Skills and Preparing for the Future Job Market

As the job market evolves, the demand for skills related to AI and data analytics is rapidly increasing. AI is not only changing the landscape of available jobs but also influencing the types of skills that are in high demand. Educational institutions are leveraging AI to help students develop the competencies needed to thrive in a technology-driven workforce.

1. Personalized Learning Pathways:

AI-driven educational platforms like Coursera, Udacity, and LinkedIn Learning offer courses tailored to individual learning goals and career aspirations. By analyzing a user's skills, preferences, and learning pace, these platforms recommend specific courses and learning paths that align with the learner's professional objectives. This personalized approach helps students acquire the skills needed for emerging job roles, such as data scientists, AI engineers, and digital marketing specialists.

2. Skill Assessment and Certification:

AI tools are also used for assessing skills and providing certifications that are recognized by employers. Platforms like Codility and HackerRank use AI to evaluate coding skills, offering challenges that test problem-solving abilities and programming knowledge. Upon completion, users receive feedback and can earn certifications that demonstrate their expertise to potential employers.

3. AI-Powered Career Guidance:

AI can help students navigate their career paths by offering personalized career advice based on their skills, interests, and market trends. For instance, tools like Pymetrics use AI to assess a user's cognitive and emotional attributes through games and recommend suitable career options. AI-driven platforms like LinkedIn also analyze user profiles and job market data to suggest potential career paths and necessary skill development.

HOW EDUCATORS CAN USE AI TO ENHANCE LEARNING EXPERIENCES

Educators play a crucial role in integrating AI technologies into the learning environment, using these tools to enhance teaching methods, personalize instruction, and improve student engagement. Here are several strategies educators can use to incorporate AI effectively:

1. Implementing AI-Powered Assessment Tools:

AI can help educators streamline the grading process by automating assessments for assignments, quizzes, and exams. Tools like Gradescope use machine learning to evaluate student submissions, providing instant feedback and saving time for educators. By automating repetitive tasks, teachers can focus more on interactive teaching and addressing individual student needs.

AI-driven assessment tools also offer insights into student performance, highlighting areas where students struggle. Educators can use this data to tailor their lessons and provide additional support to those who need it, enhancing the overall learning experience.

2. Using AI for Personalized Instruction:

AI technologies enable educators to create personalized learning experiences by adapting lessons to meet individual student needs. By analyzing student data, AI can identify learning gaps and recommend specific resources or exercises to help students improve. This approach allows educators to cater to different learning styles, ensuring that each student can progress at their own pace.

For example, in language learning, AI-powered platforms like Duolingo use adaptive algorithms to adjust the difficulty of exercises based on a learner's progress. Educators can use these platforms as supplementary tools, offering personalized practice opportunities that complement classroom instruction.

3. Enhancing Classroom Engagement with AI Tools:

AI can enhance student engagement by offering interactive and immersive learning experiences. Virtual reality (VR) and augmented reality (AR) tools powered by AI can create interactive simulations that make learning more dynamic and memorable. For instance, an AI-driven VR application can transport students to historical sites or scientific environments, offering a hands-on learning experience that goes beyond traditional textbooks.

Additionally, AI-powered chatbots can be used in the classroom to facilitate discussions, answer student questions, and provide instant feedback on assignments. These chatbots can help maintain student engagement, especially in large classes where individual attention from the teacher may be limited.

4. Incorporating AI Ethics into the Curriculum:

As AI becomes more prevalent in society, it is essential for students to understand its ethical implications. Educators can incorporate discussions on AI ethics, bias, and responsible use into their curriculum, helping students critically evaluate the impact of AI technologies. By fostering an understanding of these issues, educators prepare students to use AI responsibly and make informed decisions in their future careers.

AI is transforming education in numerous ways, from enhancing personalized learning and supporting academic research to helping students develop skills for the future job market. By leveraging AI technologies, educators can create more engaging, efficient, and tailored learning experiences. As AI continues to evolve, its potential to reshape the educational landscape will only grow, offering new opportunities for students and teachers alike.

CHAPTER 6

BUSINESS APPLICATIONS OF AI

Artificial Intelligence (AI) is reshaping the business landscape, transforming industries by automating processes, enhancing customer experiences, and enabling data-driven decision-making. From customer service to predictive analytics, AI applications are becoming central to business strategies, helping companies increase efficiency, reduce costs, and stay competitive. This chapter provides an overview of AI's role in various industries, explores key use cases, presents case studies of successful AI implementation, and offers guidance on how businesses can start incorporating AI into their strategies.

OVERVIEW OF AI IN VARIOUS INDUSTRIES

AI's versatility makes it applicable across a wide range of industries, each benefiting uniquely from its capabilities:

1. Retail:

In the retail sector, AI is used for personalized marketing, inventory management, and customer service. By analyzing customer data, AI can predict buying behavior, recommend products, and tailor marketing campaigns to individual preferences. Additionally, AI-powered chatbots and virtual assistants help businesses provide 24/7 customer support, enhancing the shopping experience.

2. Healthcare:

AI is revolutionizing healthcare by assisting in diagnostics, treatment planning, and patient care. Machine learning models analyze medical images to detect diseases like cancer with high accuracy. AI-powered virtual health assistants help patients monitor their symptoms and provide recommendations. In addition, predictive analytics in healthcare can forecast patient outcomes, enabling proactive care and improving treatment success rates.

3. Finance:

The finance industry utilizes AI for fraud detection, risk assessment, and algorithmic trading. AI algorithms analyze large datasets to identify fraudulent activities in real time, safeguarding customers and institutions. Robo-advisors use AI to provide personalized investment advice based on individual risk profiles. In trading, AI algorithms execute high-frequency trades by analyzing market trends and making decisions at lightning speed.

4. Manufacturing:

AI enhances manufacturing by optimizing production processes, reducing downtime, and improving quality control. Predictive maintenance, powered by AI, monitors equipment performance to anticipate failures before they occur, minimizing disruptions. In quality control, AI systems analyze product defects, helping manufacturers maintain high standards and reduce waste.

5. Logistics and Supply Chain:

In logistics, AI streamlines operations by optimizing route planning, inventory management, and demand forecasting. AI algorithms analyze historical data and real-time factors like weather and traffic to find the most efficient delivery routes, reducing costs and improving delivery times. AI-powered demand forecasting helps businesses predict inventory needs accurately, reducing overstocking and stockouts.

Key Use Cases of AI in Business

AI applications in business are diverse, but several key use cases stand out for their widespread adoption and significant impact:

1. Customer Service:

AI-powered customer service solutions, such as chatbots and virtual assistants, have become essential tools for businesses. Chatbots can handle routine inquiries, provide instant responses, and guide customers through simple tasks like tracking orders or resetting passwords. This automation reduces wait times and frees up human agents to handle more complex issues, improving overall customer satisfaction.

For example, companies like Sephora use AI chatbots to assist customers with product recommendations based on their preferences and previous purchases. These chatbots leverage natural language processing (NLP) to understand customer inquiries and provide personalized responses, enhancing the shopping experience.

2. Predictive Analytics:

Predictive analytics involves using AI algorithms to analyze historical data and make forecasts about future trends and behaviors. In marketing, predictive analytics helps businesses anticipate customer needs, optimize campaigns, and improve targeting. For instance, Netflix uses AI to predict which shows a user is likely to watch based on their viewing history, helping to personalize content recommendations.

In supply chain management, predictive analytics enables companies to forecast demand accurately, optimize inventory levels, and prevent stockouts. This capability is crucial for industries like retail, where customer demand can fluctuate based on seasonality, promotions, and market trends.

3. Process Automation:

Robotic Process Automation (RPA) uses AI to automate repetitive, rule-based tasks such as data entry, invoicing, and payroll processing. RPA can handle large volumes of transactions quickly and accurately, reducing the need for manual intervention and minimizing errors. This automation frees up employees to focus on more strategic and creative tasks.

For instance, financial institutions like JPMorgan Chase use AI-powered RPA to process loan applications faster. By automating the document review and verification process, banks can significantly reduce processing times, enhance accuracy, and improve customer satisfaction.

4. Decision Support:

AI-powered decision support systems (DSS) help businesses make informed decisions by analyzing data and providing actionable insights. These systems use machine learning and data analytics to identify trends, patterns, and potential risks, enabling companies to make data-driven decisions.

For example, Amazon's recommendation engine is an AI-driven decision support system that analyzes customer data to suggest products based on previous purchases, browsing history, and preferences. This approach helps increase sales and enhance the customer experience by providing personalized product suggestions.

Case Studies of Companies Successfully Implementing AI

1. Netflix – Personalized Recommendations:

Netflix is a prime example of how AI can be used to enhance customer experiences. The company uses machine learning algorithms to analyze users' viewing history and preferences, creating personalized content recommendations. This personalized approach has significantly contributed to user retention, as customers are more likely to stay engaged with the platform when they receive relevant content suggestions. Netflix's recommendation engine is estimated to save the company over $1 billion annually by reducing churn.

2. Tesla – Autonomous Driving:

Tesla is at the forefront of using AI for autonomous driving. The company's vehicles are equipped with advanced AI systems that use computer vision, machine learning, and deep learning to interpret real-time data from sensors and cameras. Tesla's Autopilot feature can perform tasks like lane-keeping, adaptive cruise control, and automatic parking, enhancing the driving experience and improving safety. Tesla's success in implementing AI in its cars has positioned the company as a leader in the autonomous vehicle industry.

3. Amazon – Supply Chain Optimization:

Amazon uses AI extensively to optimize its supply chain operations. The company employs predictive analytics to forecast demand and manage inventory levels effectively. Machine learning algorithms analyze customer data, historical sales, and external factors like weather patterns to antici-pate product demand accurately. This allows Amazon to stock its warehouses efficiently and ensure quick delivery times. The company's use of AI in logistics has been a key factor in its ability to offer same-day and next-day delivery services.

How Businesses Can Start Incorporating AI into Their Strategies

Adopting AI can seem daunting for businesses, especially those new to the technology. However, companies of all sizes can integrate AI into their operations by following a strategic approach:

1. Identify Business Needs:

The first step in incorporating AI is to identify specific business problems or areas where AI can add value. This could include improving customer service, optimizing marketing efforts, or streamlining internal processes. By pinpointing clear objectives, companies can focus their efforts on implementing AI solutions that directly address their needs.

2. Start Small with Pilot Projects:

Instead of a full-scale implementation, businesses should begin with pilot projects to test AI technologies on a smaller scale. This allows companies to experiment, gather feedback, and make adjustments without significant risk. For example, a company might deploy a chatbot on its website to handle common customer queries before expanding to more complex applications.

3. Leverage Existing AI Tools and Platforms:

Businesses do not need to build AI systems from scratch. There are numerous AI tools and platforms available that can be customized to fit specific needs. Services like Google Cloud AI, Microsoft Azure AI, and IBM Watson provide businesses with the infrastructure and tools to develop and deploy AI applications efficiently.

4. Invest in AI Skills and Training:

For successful AI adoption, companies need to invest in skills development and training for their employees. This includes hiring data scientists, AI specialists, and software developers with expertise in machine learning. Additionally, providing training to existing staff on how to use AI tools and interpret data analytics is essential for integrating AI into daily business operations.

5. Focus on Data Quality:

AI relies heavily on high-quality data to produce accurate insights. Companies must ensure they have robust data management practices in place to collect, clean, and organize data effectively. Implementing data governance policies and using data analytics tools can help businesses maintain the integrity and accuracy of their data.

6. Monitor and Evaluate Performance:

Once AI solutions are implemented, it is crucial to monitor their performance continuously. Businesses should track key performance indicators (KPIs) and assess whether the AI applications are meeting their objectives. Regular evaluation allows companies to make necessary adjustments, optimize processes, and maximize the benefits of their AI investments.

AI is transforming the business world, offering innovative solutions that drive efficiency, enhance customer experiences, and provide valuable insights. By understanding the key use cases and successful implementations of AI, businesses can identify opportunities to integrate these technologies into their operations. Starting with pilot projects, leveraging existing tools, and investing in skills development can help companies adopt AI strategically, positioning them for long-term success in a rapidly evolving market.

CHAPTER 7

How to Approach AI as an Individual

Artificial Intelligence (AI) is no longer a concept confined to research labs and tech giants; it is now a part of our everyday lives. Whether we realize it or not, AI influences everything from the way we interact online to the decisions we make based on recommendations from algorithms. As AI continues to evolve, individuals must equip themselves with the knowledge and skills to navigate this rapidly changing landscape effectively. This chapter explores how to stay informed about AI, offers resources for further learning, and discusses how to engage responsibly with AI technologies.

Tips for Staying Informed and Understanding AI's Impact on Your Field

1. Identify AI Trends in Your Industry:

The impact of AI varies significantly across industries. For instance, in healthcare, AI is transforming diagnostics and patient care through predictive analytics and medical imaging. In finance, AI is reshaping fraud detection and investment strategies. In retail, it powers personalized recommendations and customer service chatbots. Understanding how AI is being applied in your field can provide insights into emerging trends and opportunities.

To stay informed, regularly read industry-specific publications and reports that highlight the latest developments in AI. Websites like MIT Technology Review, Wired, and TechCrunch often feature in-depth analyses of AI trends. Additionally, many industries have dedicated conferences and events, such as the AI in Healthcare Summit or AI in Retail Conference, where experts discuss current applications and future directions. Attending such events, either in person or virtually, can help you gain a better understanding of how AI is shaping your industry.

2. Follow Key AI Thought Leaders and Organizations:

Another effective way to stay updated on AI developments is by following thought leaders, researchers, and organizations at the forefront of AI research and implementation. Notable figures like Andrew Ng, Fei-Fei Li, and Elon Musk often share their insights on the future of AI and its societal implications. Similarly, companies like OpenAI, Google DeepMind, and IBM Watson frequently publish research papers and articles that shed light on cutting-edge AI technologies.

Engaging with these voices on platforms like Twitter, LinkedIn, and Medium can provide you with regular updates on AI advancements. Many thought leaders also offer newsletters or blogs that compile the latest research findings and industry news, making it easier for you to stay informed.

3. Participate in Online Communities and Forums:

Online communities and forums can be valuable resources for staying informed about AI. Platforms like Reddit's r/MachineLearning and r/ArtificialIntelligence, as well as specialized forums like the AI section of Stack Overflow, allow you to engage with other enthusiasts, ask questions, and share knowledge. These communities often discuss recent breakthroughs, practical applications, and ethical considerations in AI, providing a space for ongoing learning and dialogue.

Additionally, joining professional groups on LinkedIn related to AI and data science can connect you with industry professionals who share valuable insights and resources. Engaging in discussions and networking with others interested in AI can help you keep pace with the latest developments and expand your understanding of the field.

Resources for Learning More About AI

1. Online Courses and Certifications:

With the increasing availability of online education, there are numerous courses and certification programs designed to teach individuals about AI, regardless of their prior knowledge level. Platforms like Coursera, edX, Udacity, and LinkedIn Learning offer a variety of AI courses, from beginner to advanced levels.

- Introduction to AI: Courses like Elements of AI by the University of Helsinki provide a beginner-friendly overview of AI concepts without requiring technical expertise.
- Machine Learning Specializations: If you want a deeper understanding, you might consider taking Andrew Ng's Machine Learning course on Coursera, which covers foundational concepts and algorithms.
- AI for Everyone: For a broader audience, AI for Everyone by Andrew Ng focuses on non-technical aspects of AI, providing insights into its business applications and societal impact.

Earning certifications from reputable platforms can help you build credibility and demonstrate your understanding of AI concepts, making it easier to leverage AI in your career.

2. Books and Publications:

Reading books written by experts in the field can provide a comprehensive understanding of AI, its history, and its potential future. Some highly recommended titles include:

- Artificial Intelligence: A Guide for Thinking Humans by Melanie Mitchell: This book offers an accessible introduction to AI, discussing its capabilities and limitations.
- Life 3.0: Being Human in the Age of Artificial Intelligence by Max Tegmark: This book explores the impact of AI on society and the future of humanity.
- Superintelligence: Paths, Dangers, Strategies by Nick Bostrom: This book delves into the potential risks and ethical challenges posed by advanced AI systems.

Additionally, subscribing to reputable journals and magazines like the Journal of Artificial Intelligence Research or IEEE Spectrum can keep you up-to-date with the latest research and developments in the field.

3. Podcasts and Videos:

For those who prefer audio or visual learning, podcasts and YouTube channels can be great sources of information. Popular AI podcasts like The AI Alignment Podcast, Lex Fridman Podcast, and AI Today feature interviews with experts and discussions on AI trends, ethical issues, and future possibilities. YouTube channels like Two Minute Papers and CrashCourse AI offer informative videos that break down complex AI topics into easily digestible content.

How to Engage Responsibly with AI Technology

1. Be Aware of Ethical Considerations:

As an individual engaging with AI, it is crucial to be aware of the ethical implications of using AI technologies. Issues such as bias, privacy, and transparency are central to responsible AI usage. For instance, facial recognition systems have been criticized for their lack of accuracy and potential biases against certain demographic groups. When using AI tools, it is essential to understand how they work and consider the potential consequences of their use.

Before adopting an AI tool, research its underlying algorithms, data sources, and ethical guidelines. Choose tools developed by companies that prioritize fairness, accountability, and transparency in their AI systems. Additionally, be mindful of data privacy and avoid using AI applications that may compromise your personal information.

2. Understand AI's Limitations:

AI systems, despite their capabilities, have limitations. They are designed to recognize patterns in data and make predictions based on that data but may struggle in unfamiliar contexts or with unexpected inputs. For example, while AI can excel in specific tasks like image recognition, it may fail in tasks requiring complex reasoning or common sense.

When using AI tools, it is essential to understand that they are not infallible and can produce incorrect or biased outputs. Always verify the results of AI applications, especially when making important decisions based on their recommendations. This awareness will help you use AI effectively while mitigating potential risks.

3. Advocate for Transparency and Fairness:

As an AI user, you can contribute to responsible AI development by advocating for transparency and fairness. Support companies and organizations that commit to ethical AI practices, such as minimizing bias in their algorithms and providing clear explanations of how their AI systems work. By choosing ethical AI products, you help promote responsible innovation.

Additionally, if you notice biases or inaccuracies in an AI tool, report them to the developers. Providing feedback can help improve the system and make it more reliable and equitable. Engaging in discussions about AI ethics and raising awareness about potential issues can also contribute to the development of more fair and accountable AI technologies.

4. Stay Curious and Adaptable:

The field of AI is evolving rapidly, and new tools, applications, and ethical challenges are emerging regularly. To engage effectively with AI, maintain a curious mindset and be open to learning. Embrace opportunities to experiment with new AI technologies, whether it's using a virtual assistant to organize your schedule or exploring AI-powered creativity tools.

Keeping an adaptable attitude will enable you to take advantage of AI's potential while remaining vigilant about its limitations and risks. Staying informed, learning continuously, and actively participating in conversations about AI will empower you to navigate the AI-driven world responsibly and confidently.

Approaching AI as an individual requires a proactive mindset, a commitment to continuous learning, and an ethical approach to technology use. By staying informed about AI trends, utilizing educational resources, and engaging responsibly with AI tools, you can harness the power of AI in your personal and professional life. As AI continues to transform industries and reshape our society, individuals equipped with the right knowledge and skills will be better positioned to leverage these technologies effectively and responsibly.

Afterword

As we conclude this journey into understanding artificial intelligence (AI), it is clear that AI has moved from being a futuristic concept to an integral part of our daily lives. Through this book, we have explored what AI is, delved into its rich history, examined its current state, and looked into its numerous applications across personal, educational, and business contexts. We have seen how AI has evolved from early speculative ideas to powerful, sophisticated systems capable of transforming industries and reshaping societal norms.

One of the key takeaways is the sheer variety of AI technologies available today. From simple recommendation algorithms to complex deep learning models, AI has a wide range of capabilities that can solve problems, enhance productivity, and offer personalized experiences. Understanding the distinctions between AI, machine learning, and data science is crucial, as each plays a unique role in how intelligent systems are developed and utilized. While AI is the overarching field, machine learning focuses on algorithms that learn from data, and deep learning, a subset of machine learning, uses neural networks to model and predict complex patterns.

The history of AI is marked by periods of rapid progress, significant breakthroughs, and occasional setbacks known as "AI winters." However, the resilience of researchers and the growing interest in AI's potential have led to a revival of interest, particularly in the 21st century. Today, we see AI's impact in natural language processing, image recognition, robotics, and various other fields. Companies like OpenAI, Google DeepMind, and IBM Watson are leading the charge, pushing the boundaries of what AI can achieve.

The real-world applications of AI are extensive. On a personal level, AI enhances our daily activities through voice assistants, recommendation systems, and smart home devices. In education, AI-driven platforms offer personalized learning experiences and academic support, preparing students for a tech-driven job market. In business, AI is transforming customer service, optimizing supply chains, and providing powerful tools for decision-making. These diverse use cases demonstrate AI's versatility and its potential to drive significant changes in multiple areas of our lives.

However, with great power comes great responsibility. As AI continues to integrate into various facets of society, it is essential to consider its ethical implications. Issues like bias in AI algorithms, privacy concerns, and the need for transparency in AI decision-making are becoming increasingly important. Responsible AI use is not just about leveraging technology effectively; it also involves understanding and mitigating potential risks. Engaging with AI responsibly means being aware of these challenges, advocating for fairness and accountability, and making informed choices when using AI tools.

The journey of understanding AI does not end here. This field is continuously evolving, with new developments, opportunities, and challenges emerging regularly. For individuals, staying informed and continuously learning about AI is essential to remain adaptable in a rapidly changing technological landscape. Whether you are an industry professional looking to integrate AI into your work, an educator exploring ways to enhance learning experiences, or simply someone curious about the future of technology, there are countless resources available to deepen your knowledge.

In conclusion, AI has the potential to be a transformative force for good, but its impact depends on how we choose to engage with it. By approaching AI with a willingness to learn, a commitment to ethical practices, and an open mind towards its possibilities, we can harness its power to create a better, more efficient, and equitable future. The exploration of AI is just beginning, and the next steps you take in this journey can shape not only your understanding but also the world around you. Embrace the challenge, continue learning, and be a part of the conversation that will define the future of artificial intelligence.

References and Citations

The information provided throughout the chapters of this book draws from a variety of reputable sources, offering a broad perspective on artificial intelligence (AI), its history, applications, and societal implications. Below is a list of key references and citations used to gather the insights presented.

1. Russell, S., & Norvig, P. (2010). Artificial Intelligence: A Modern Approach (3rd ed.). Prentice Hall.

- This comprehensive textbook provided foundational knowledge on AI definitions, machine learning, and neural networks. It is a leading resource in the field, covering everything from basic concepts to advanced algorithms.

2. Goodfellow, I., Bengio, Y., & Courville, A. (2016). Deep Learning. MIT Press.

- The book offered a detailed explanation of deep learning and its significance within the broader AI landscape, including discussions on neural networks and the advancements in AI technologies.

3. Domingos, P. (2015). The Master Algorithm: How the Quest for the Ultimate Learning Machine Will Remake Our World. Basic Books.

- This resource was instrumental in exploring the evolution of machine learning and the different paradigms within AI, helping to clarify the differences between AI, machine learning, and data science.

4. Tegmark, M. (2017). Life 3.0: Being Human in the Age of Artificial Intelligence. Knopf.

- Max Tegmark's book provided a forward-looking perspective on AI's potential impact on society, including ethical considerations and the future of AI development.

5. Bostrom, N. (2014). Superintelligence: Paths, Dangers, Strategies. Oxford University Press.

- This text was used to discuss the potential risks of advanced AI systems and the importance of responsible AI development, particularly in the context of AI safety and ethical concerns.

6. Marr, B. (2020). Artificial Intelligence in Practice: How 50 Successful Companies Used AI and Machine Learning to Solve Problems. Wiley.

- This book offered practical insights and case studies of companies successfully implementing AI in various industries, providing real-world examples for the business applications of AI.

7. Haenlein, M., & Kaplan, A. (2019). "A Brief History of Artificial Intelligence: On the Past, Present, and Future of Artificial Intelligence." California Management Review, 61(4), 5–14.

- This article provided an overview of AI's history, including significant milestones, AI winters, and recent revivals, which were essential in understanding the evolution of the field.

8. Online Learning Platforms: Coursera, edX, and Udacity

- These platforms were referenced as educational resources where readers can find courses on AI, machine learning, and data science to further their understanding of the subject.

9. Industry Reports: McKinsey & Company, PwC, and Gartner

- Reports from these consulting firms provided insights into current AI technologies, industry trends, and predictions about the future state of AI, particularly in business and educational contexts.

10. OpenAI and Google DeepMind Research Publications

- The latest research papers and articles from these leading AI research organizations were used to gather information on cutting-edge developments in AI, such as advancements in natural language processing and robotics.

11. Mitchell, M. (2019). Artificial Intelligence: A Guide for Thinking Humans. Farrar, Straus and Giroux.

- Melanie Mitchell's book contributed to the explanation of complex AI concepts in accessible terms, which was useful for introducing key topics in the initial chapters of the book.

12. Podcasts and Online Resources: Lex Fridman Podcast, AI Alignment Podcast, and MIT Technology Review

- These sources provided contemporary insights and expert interviews that informed discussions on the current state of AI, as well as ethical and societal impacts.